CONTENTS

Scripture taken from the HOLY BIBLE, NEW INTERNATIONAL VERSION®.
Copyright © 1973, 1978, 1984 by International Bible Society.
Used by permission of Zondervan Publishing House.
All rights reserved.

The "NIV" and "New International Version" trademarks are registered in the
United States Patent and Trademark Office by International Bible Society.
Use of either trademark requires the permission of International Bible Society.

The Standard Publishing Company, Cincinnati, Ohio
A division of Standex International Corporation

01 00 99 98 97 96 95 94   5 4 3 2 1

ISBN #0-7847-0055-9

CRAFTS JUST FOR FUN

CRAFT TIME = FUN TIME for kids, but what about adults?

First, you find the project. Then you collect the *stuff. Stuff* means paint and brushes, . . . paper and scissors, . . . glue and tape, . . . markers and pencils . . . and the list goes on.

Second step: How does it work? So, you make up the model. You show it to the kids and you give directions—maybe two or three times. Then you help the kids "create" something that may or may not resemble the original model.

And last but not least, you clean up the mess.

The BIG QUESTION is this: Are crafts worth it? Do they do more than fill the gap between snack time and closing? Are they more than a cheap substitute for video games? The answer is YES!

Crafts teach
- *teamwork* in sharing materials, tools and space,
- *independence* in work skills,
- *discipline* of completing a project, and
- *responsibility* for materials, tools and cleanup.

Crafts develop
- *confidence*—"I did it myself,"
- *creativity*—there is no "right" way,
- *enjoyment* of simple, inexpensive activities, and
- basic *physical skills.*

Crafts bring to mind
- a happy place—church,
- a special person—teacher,
- a story or Scripture verse,
- God, and
- the plan of salvation.

Why do crafts? Crafts reinforce lessons and help children retain what they have learned in class. Crafts continue to teach long after the project is over. So teach. Encourage. Create a memory . . . with crafts.

3

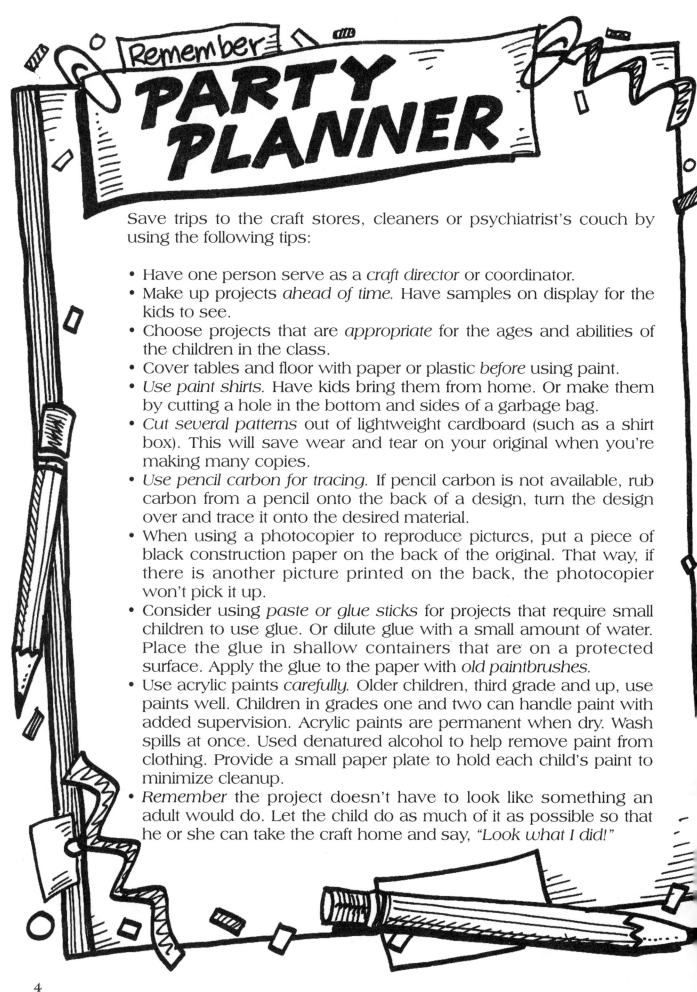

Remember PARTY PLANNER

Save trips to the craft stores, cleaners or psychiatrist's couch by using the following tips:

- Have one person serve as a *craft director* or coordinator.
- Make up projects *ahead of time.* Have samples on display for the kids to see.
- Choose projects that are *appropriate* for the ages and abilities of the children in the class.
- Cover tables and floor with paper or plastic *before* using paint.
- *Use paint shirts.* Have kids bring them from home. Or make them by cutting a hole in the bottom and sides of a garbage bag.
- *Cut several patterns* out of lightweight cardboard (such as a shirt box). This will save wear and tear on your original when you're making many copies.
- *Use pencil carbon for tracing.* If pencil carbon is not available, rub carbon from a pencil onto the back of a design, turn the design over and trace it onto the desired material.
- When using a photocopier to reproduce pictures, put a piece of black construction paper on the back of the original. That way, if there is another picture printed on the back, the photocopier won't pick it up.
- Consider using *paste or glue sticks* for projects that require small children to use glue. Or dilute glue with a small amount of water. Place the glue in shallow containers that are on a protected surface. Apply the glue to the paper with *old paintbrushes.*
- Use acrylic paints *carefully.* Older children, third grade and up, use paints well. Children in grades one and two can handle paint with added supervision. Acrylic paints are permanent when dry. Wash spills at once. Used denatured alcohol to help remove paint from clothing. Provide a small paper plate to hold each child's paint to minimize cleanup.
- *Remember* the project doesn't have to look like something an adult would do. Let the child do as much of it as possible so that he or she can take the craft home and say, *"Look what I did!"*

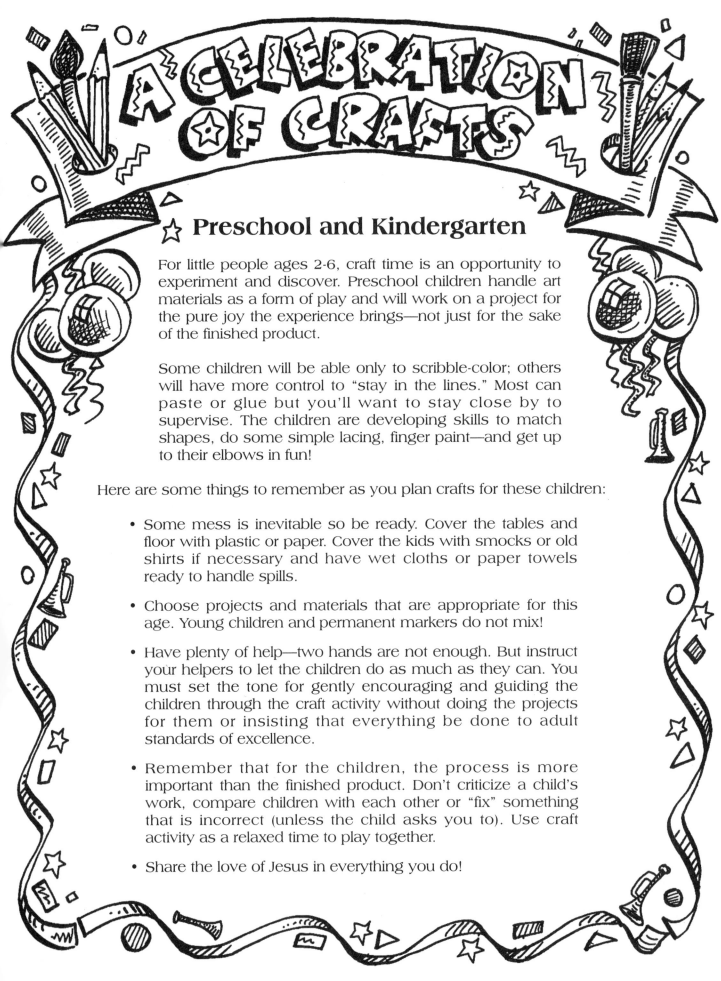

A CELEBRATION OF CRAFTS

☆ Preschool and Kindergarten

For little people ages 2-6, craft time is an opportunity to experiment and discover. Preschool children handle art materials as a form of play and will work on a project for the pure joy the experience brings—not just for the sake of the finished product.

Some children will be able only to scribble-color; others will have more control to "stay in the lines." Most can paste or glue but you'll want to stay close by to supervise. The children are developing skills to match shapes, do some simple lacing, finger paint—and get up to their elbows in fun!

Here are some things to remember as you plan crafts for these children:

- Some mess is inevitable so be ready. Cover the tables and floor with plastic or paper. Cover the kids with smocks or old shirts if necessary and have wet cloths or paper towels ready to handle spills.

- Choose projects and materials that are appropriate for this age. Young children and permanent markers do not mix!

- Have plenty of help—two hands are not enough. But instruct your helpers to let the children do as much as they can. You must set the tone for gently encouraging and guiding the children through the craft activity without doing the projects for them or insisting that everything be done to adult standards of excellence.

- Remember that for the children, the process is more important than the finished product. Don't criticize a child's work, compare children with each other or "fix" something that is incorrect (unless the child asks you to). Use craft activity as a relaxed time to play together.

- Share the love of Jesus in everything you do!

Party Accessories

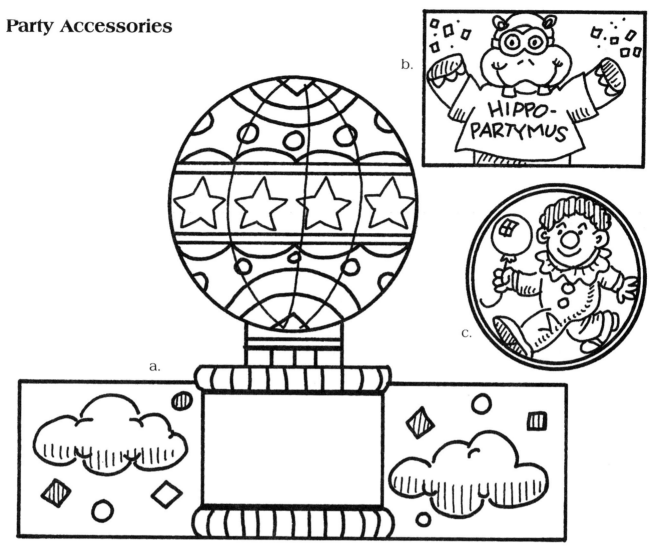

b.

HIPPO-PARTYMUS

c.

a.

Materials
- Art for nut cup wrapper (a), art for napkin ring (b), art for place card (c) traced or copied.
- Nut cup for each student; colored index card cut in half vertically or 3" x 5" piece of construction paper; strip of construction paper approximately 2" x 5½"
- Napkins
- Glue, paste, and tape
- Scissors
- Crayons

Here's How
- Let the children color the art. Cut out the pieces.
- Use 2" x 5½" strip of construction paper for a napkin ring.
- Show the child how to wrap the strip around his napkin and glue the clown on (see d).
- Fold the index card or construction paper so it will stand up for a place card. Let the child glue Hippo-Partymus on the card. Print child's name (see e).
- Show the child how to fasten the hot air balloon around the nut cup and tape. Print the child's name (see f).

d.

e.

f.

Follow Jesus Megaphone

Materials
- Copy of party paper from page 8
- Crayons
- Tape
- Scissors
- Chenille wire
- Punch

Here's How
- Punch a hole on each cross.
- Have the child color the paper.
- Help the child form a handle from his chenille wire.
- Poke it through the holes you have punched at the crosses.
- Secure the ends with tape on the underneath side.
- Trim the edges and help him roll the paper into a megaphone. Tape securely.

Party Hat

Materials
- Pieces of cute wrapping paper, newspaper, or wallpaper (12" x 18" for each child)
- Tape
- Crepe paper streamers (optional)

Here's How
- Help the child fold his paper in half to 9" x 12".
- Fold the folded corners into the center so they meet, forming a triangle. Fasten with tape.
- Fold the open edges up; open the hat.
- Child will wear hat and march around the room waving his streamers.

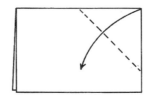 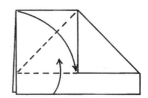

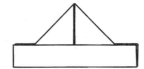

Happy/Sad Clown

UBS95

Materials
- Copies of parts of happy clown (page 9) and sad clown (page 10)
- Paper plates
- Dowel rods
- Crayons or markers
- Glue or paste; tape
- Scissors
- Yarn (optional)

Here's How
- Let the child color the parts of the happy clown.
- Cut them out. Help him place them on the front of his paper plate. Glue in place.
- Repeat the procedure for the sad clown and place on the back of the paper plate.
- Outline the mouth with yarn (optional).
- Add other touch-and-feel materials.
- Tape a dowel rod onto the plate to form a two-faced puppet.

Party Invitation

Materials
- Copies of party invitations from page 11
- Crayons
- Scissors or X-acto knife
- Envelopes (optional)

Here's How
- Cut on dotted lines so that the words "Celebrate Jesus" will pop out when card is opened.
- Assist the child in folding the card into fourths using the cross as a guide.
- Child will color front and inside of card.

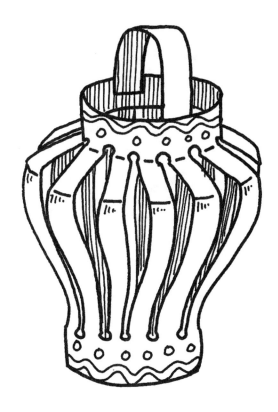

Party Lantern

Materials
- Two-toned construction paper (9" x 12")
- Paper punches
- Rulers
- Pencils
- Scissors
- Sequins
- Rickrack
- Crayons or markers
- Glue or paste

Here's How
- Cut a ½" strip from long side of paper for handle.
- Using a ruler mark lines ½" apart, leaving 1 inch at top and bottom. Cut on lines.
- At the top and bottom of each slit, punch a small hole to keep slits from tearing out.
- Assist child in rolling the lantern vertically and pasting or gluing sides overlapping slightly.
- Child may color design around top and bottom, add sequins and rickrack.
- Print "Celebrate Jesus" on lantern.

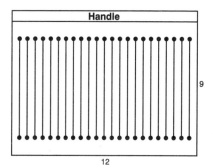

Handle

9

12

Stuffed Hot Air Balloon

Materials
- For each child, two copies of balloon and two copies of gondola from page 13
- Yarn (64" per child)
- Stuffing material (such as tissue, cotton, old pantyhose)
- Crayons
- Paper punches
- Scissors

Here's How
- Cut balloons and gondolas.
- Child may color balloons and gondolas.
- Punch holes near edges of front and back of balloon and gondola (matching fronts and backs).
- Child will use yarn (tip in glue or nail polish, then twist tip into point and allow to dry) to lace the balloon and gondola. (When he has done most of them, let him stuff them, then continue lacing.
- Assist child in cutting pieces of yarn to attach the gondola to the balloon.

**Stuffed
Hot Air Balloon**

13

**Hippo-
Partymus
Puppet**

(See page 15
for instructions.)

Instructions for
Hippo-Partymus Puppet
(Page 14)

Materials
- Copy of parts from page 14
- Glue
- Paper lunch bags
- Scissors
- Crayons

Here's How
- Child will color all parts of the puppet.
- Cut out parts and assist child in gluing them onto the paper bag as shown.

Turnaround
Clown

(See page 16 for instructions.)

Turnaround Clown

Materials
- Copies of Turnaround Clown (front—page 15; back—this page)
- Scissors
- Crayons
- Paper fasteners

Here's How
- Cut out face of Turnaround Clown from page 15 and back from this page.
- Child will color the clown.
- Assemble the clown by pushing paper fastener through the center of both parts. Tape the fastener so child will not be injured.

BOUNCING PARTY PERSON

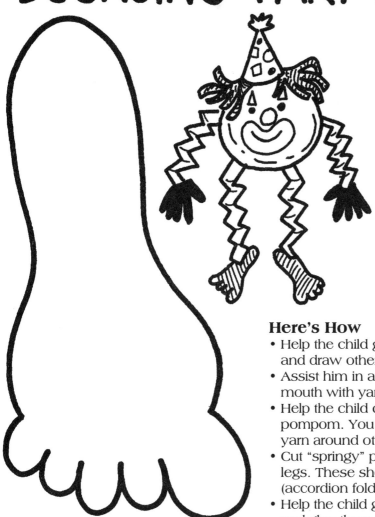

Materials
- Two hands, two feet, and mouth for each child made from pattern—we suggest using black construction paper for hands and feet and red for mouth.
- Paper plates
- Construction paper
- Crayons or markers
- Glue or paste
- Yarn
- Scissors
- Pompoms

Here's How
- Help the child glue the mouth of clown on his paper plate and draw other facial features.
- Assist him in adding yarn hair—he may also outline the mouth with yarn.
- Help the child cut a triangle of paper into a hat and add a pompom. You can make the pompom by tying a piece of yarn around other pieces of yarn (see illustration).
- Cut "springy" pieces of construction paper for arms and legs. These should be 1" wide and about 20" long (accordion folded every inch).
- Help the child glue his hands and feet onto the "springs" and glue them in the proper position to make the bouncing party person.

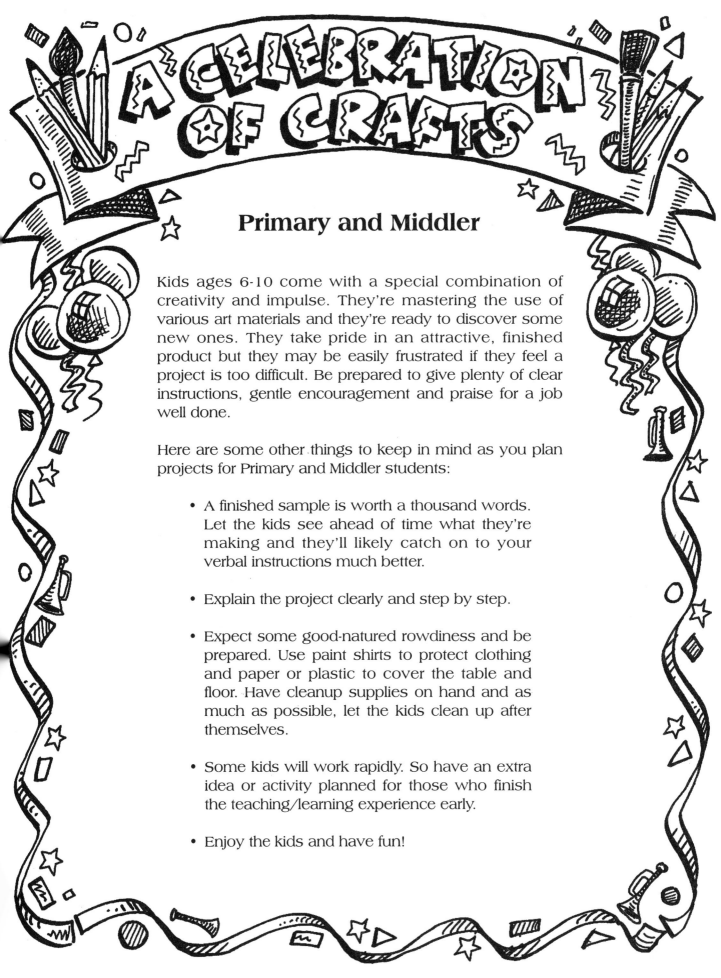

A CELEBRATION OF CRAFTS

Primary and Middler

Kids ages 6-10 come with a special combination of creativity and impulse. They're mastering the use of various art materials and they're ready to discover some new ones. They take pride in an attractive, finished product but they may be easily frustrated if they feel a project is too difficult. Be prepared to give plenty of clear instructions, gentle encouragement and praise for a job well done.

Here are some other things to keep in mind as you plan projects for Primary and Middler students:

- A finished sample is worth a thousand words. Let the kids see ahead of time what they're making and they'll likely catch on to your verbal instructions much better.

- Explain the project clearly and step by step.

- Expect some good-natured rowdiness and be prepared. Use paint shirts to protect clothing and paper or plastic to cover the table and floor. Have cleanup supplies on hand and as much as possible, let the kids clean up after themselves.

- Some kids will work rapidly. So have an extra idea or activity planned for those who finish the teaching/learning experience early.

- Enjoy the kids and have fun!

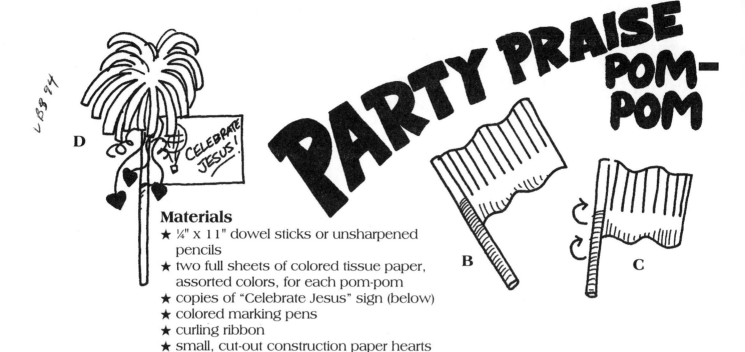

PARTY PRAISE POM-POM

Materials

★ ¼" x 11" dowel sticks or unsharpened pencils
★ two full sheets of colored tissue paper, assorted colors, for each pom-pom
★ copies of "Celebrate Jesus" sign (below)
★ colored marking pens
★ curling ribbon
★ small, cut-out construction paper hearts
★ transparent tape, scissors, glue

Here's How

1. For each pom-pom the student will need to choose two sheets of tissue paper. Use different colors.

2. Put the sheets of paper together so the corners line up. Keeping the sheets together, fold them in half, then in half again.

3. Place the folded paper on a flat surface. Carefully cut strips about ½" wide. Stop cutting about 3" below the fold. (See illustration A.)

4. Place a dowel or pencil on the paper so that one end extends over the uncut area of the tissue. (See illustration B.) Use tape to fasten the edge of the uncut area to the stick.

5. Roll the paper around the stick, as tightly as possible. Tape the rolled edge securely to the stick. The edges will not line up exactly after it is rolled. (See illustration C.)

6. Spread out the fringe so it looks good.

7. Color the "Celebrate Jesus" sign. Wrap it around the stick below the pom-pom. Glue the two halves together. Tie lengths of ribbon around the stick. Curl some ends of the ribbon. Glue construction paper hearts to other ends. (See illustration D.)

Compose a praise cheer to Jesus or say a Bible verse of praise as you use your pom-poms.

HiPPO-PARTYMUS NOTE HOLDER

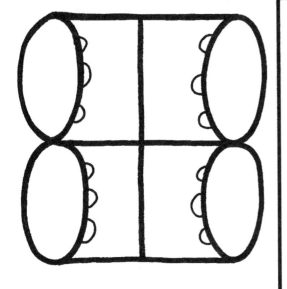

Cut this shelf piece from ⅜" wood.

Materials
★ wood (⅛" and ⅜" thick)
★ sandpaper ★ glue
★ transfer paper ★ paint
★ small squares of paper or Post-It® notes
Optional: wooden spring clothespin

Here's How
1. Using the patterns provided, cut and sand pieces of wood. All pieces are cut from ⅛" wood except for the shelf piece, which is to be cut from ⅜" wood. Paint all pieces a solid color.
2. Use transfer paper to trace the designs on the face, hooves, and bow tie. Paint these features as desired.
3. Glue the pieces together as illustrated, placing the ⅜" piece of wood under the bow tie to form a pencil shelf.
4. Glue a pad of Post-It® notes beneath the bow tie.

Option: A spring clothespin may be glued behind the head and bow tie in place of the shelf piece. Small squares of paper may then be clipped in the clothespin.

Write a note of praise about Jesus. Remember to pass it on!

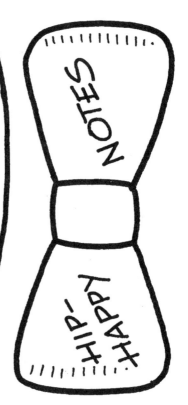

NOTES

HIP-HAPPY

HAPPY DAY

POTPOURRI MAGNET

Materials
★ empty jar lids (Peanut butter jar lids or canning jar rings with lids work well.)
★ moveable eyes   ★ netting
★ small pompons   ★ potpourri
★ scraps of felt   ★ yarn
★ adhesive-backed magnetic strip
★ rubber bands

Here's How
1. Cut a circle of netting about 2" larger than the jar lid you will be using.
2. Fill the jar lid with potpourri. Cover with the piece of netting and secure by wrapping a rubberband tightly around the edge of the lid.
3. Use the felt, eyes, pompons and yarn to create a clown face or other design. Glue pieces in place.
4 Cut a 1" piece of magnetic strip and place on back.

Your Happy Day Potpourri Magnet can remind you of the joy you have when you give to Jesus.

PARTY PRAISER

Materials
★ party hats (Purchase hats without lettering.)
★ wooden paint paddles   ★ paint and brushes
★ crepe paper or ruffled trim   ★ squares of paper
★ yarn

Here's How

1. Drill a small hole in the top of the paint paddle. Paint the paddle as desired.

2. Remove the elastic string from a party hat. Turn the hat upside down. Glue or staple the bottom edge of the hat to the paint paddle.

3. Glue gathered crepe paper or ruffled trim around the edge of the hat.

4. Thread a piece of yarn through the drilled hole and tie at the top to form a hanger for your Party Praiser.

Write Bible verses of praise or promises from God on small slips of paper. Fold the papers and put them into the hat. Hang your Party Praiser at home. Remember to pull out and read one verse each day. Thank God for His promises and smile with praise.

Follow Jesus
VBS 95

3-D MINI PLAQUE

Materials
★ wood (⅛" thick)
★ copies of the "Jesus" fish art from this page
★ paint and brushes
★ glue
★ clear acryllic spray paint or shellac
★ *Optional:* permanent marking pens

Here's How

1. Using the patterns provided, cut and sand the three tiers and two easel pieces.

2. Paint the three tiers as desired. When dry, glue them together, placing the largest at the bottom and smallest one on top.

3. Cut out the fish art. Color, if desired, and glue it to the front of the plaque.

4. Glue the short edges of the two easels to the back of the plaque to make the plaque stand.

5. Spray clear acrylic paint or paint a thin layer of shellac over the top of the plaque to give it a nice finish.

Set your finished mini plaque on a knickknack shelf at home.
Be sure to remember and obey Jesus' words in John 21:19: "Follow me."

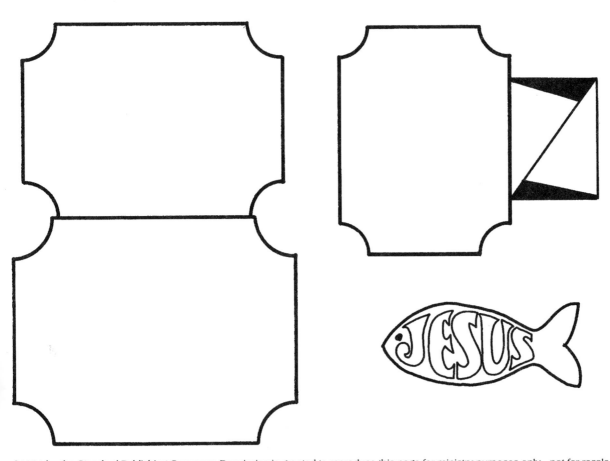

Hip·Hippo·Ray
Name Card
&
Favor

Materials
★ copies of the Hip·Hippo·Ray Name Card from this page
★ colored marking pens
★ balloons or individually-wrapped candies
★ tape
★ glue
★ scissors

Here's How
1. For each name card, cut out and color the card and inside message. Be sure to cut the small slit at the bottom of the hippo's face.

2. Write a name on the line provided on the front of the card.

3. Fold the card and glue the message inside. Tape a balloon or piece of wrapped candy on the inside.

4. Fold the bottom stand and insert the tab through the slit on the front of the card. Stand one card at each place setting.

Kids will enjoy finding the surprise inside and can use the name cards as daily reminders of the joy Jesus gives each day.

Have A 'Hip·Hippo·Ray' Day with JESUS!

24

Curly Top
Treasure Keeper

Materials

★ assortment of empty jars with lids (baby food jars, shortening cans, potato chip containers)
★ scraps of felt, lace, rickrack, buttons, etc.
★ gift ribbon, curling ribbon, gift wrap
★ permanent ink marking pens
★ embroidery thread and needle
★ paint and brushes
★ moveable eyes
★ construction paper
★ glue

Here's How

1. Paint the lid of a container. Allow to dry. Cut small, tightly curled pieces of ribbon and glue them to the lid to create "hair" for your treasurer keeper.

2. "Dress" the treasure keeper by gluing lengths of gift ribbon or wrapping paper around the container. Add lace, buttons, a bow tie, etc., as desired.

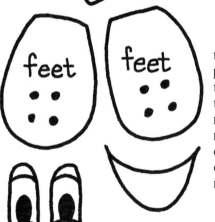

3. Make facial features at the top of the container. Use the patterns given on this page. Cut the pieces from felt and glue them onto your container. You may choose to glue on moveable eyes or make your own facial design on the container with permanent marking pens.

Use your Treasure Keeper to collect coins for a missions offering, or fill it with nuts and candies to share with others. Remember that nothing is too much or too little to give to Jesus.

Materials

★ wood (⅛"thick)
★ sandpaper
★ paint and brushes
★ poster board
★ yarn
★ transfer paper
★ copies of Hip-Hippo-Ray sign
★ colored marking pens
★ tape, glue

"Hip-Hippo-Ray" Peekover Room Sign

Here's How

1. Using the patterns provided, cut wood pieces for the hippo's face, arms, and legs. Sand.

2. Paint the pieces a solid color. When dry, use transfer paper to trace the facial features and hoof prints. Paint features as desired.

3. Cut a piece of poster board 3½" x 7". Color the Hip-Hippo-Ray sign and glue it to the poster board.

4. Glue the painted wood pieces to the sign as illustrated. Cut a 2" piece of yarn, fold it in half to form a loop, and tape it to the back of the sign for a hanger.

Personalize your name sign and hang it on your bedroom door at home. The sign will remind you and others that one of God's kids lives there.

"LOGGIN' FOR JESUS"
Praise Journal

Materials

★ wood (⅛" thick)
★ sandpaper
★ copies of Jesus cover art (or other pictures for cover) and several copies of the Praise Page (page 28) for each journal
★ ribbon or yarn
★ leather or felt for hinges
★ paint, brushes
★ spray shellac
★ colored pencils

Here's How

1. For each front cover, cut one piece of wood 7½" x 7¾" and a second piece ¾" x 7¾". For the back cover, cut one piece of wood 8¼" x 7¾".

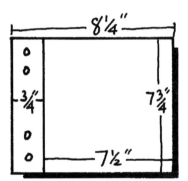

Drill four holes in the front strip and back piece as illustrated. Sand all pieces of wood.

2. Color the picture of Jesus with colored pencils or cut other pictures to fit the front cover.

(*Note:* Full-color bulletin covers are an excellent source for pictures.)

Art by Jerry Allison
©1991 S.P.Co.

3. Coat the back of the picture with glue and place it on the wood book cover. Allow to dry. Spray the notebook cover and back on all sides with spray shellac. Allow to dry. With fine sandpaper, sand over the area of the picture. Spray with another coat of shellac. Continue this process (sanding, spraying, drying) until the picture seems to melt into the wood. The more coats you use, the better it will look.

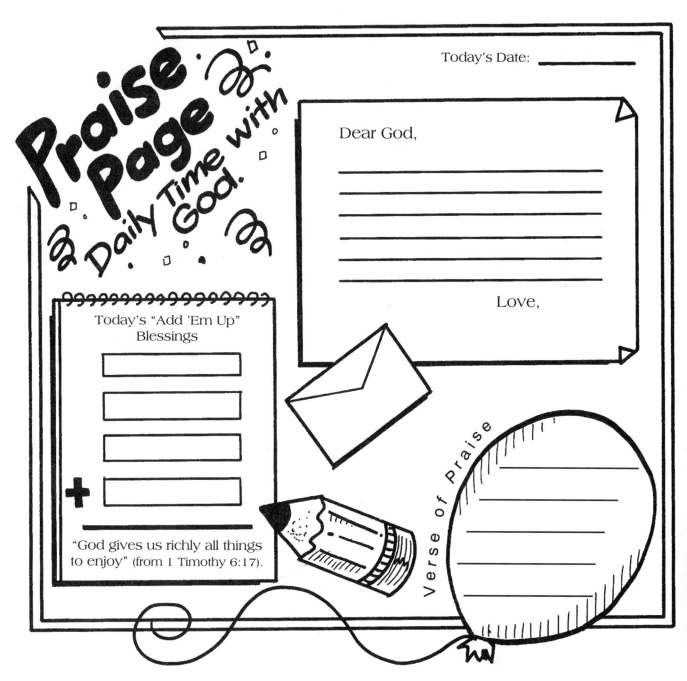

Today's Date: _____

Dear God,

_____

_____

_____

_____

_____

Love,

Today's "Add 'Em Up"
Blessings

+
_____

"God gives us richly all things
to enjoy" (from 1 Timothy 6:17).

Verse of Praise

4. To make hinges, cut out and place the hinge patterns below on a piece of leather or felt. Draw around them with a pencil and cut out.

Carefully align the wood sections of the front cover. Spread glue on the backs of hinges. Place the hinges across the two sections of the front cover as illustrated. Be sure that half the hinge is on each section of the cover. Allow glue to dry thoroughly.

5. To assemble, use a paper punch to make holes in the Praise Pages to align with the drilled holes on the cover. Place the back cover of the notebook on the table with the Praise Pages and front cover on top.

Cut two lengths of ribbon or yarn. Run the first piece of ribbon down through the top hole, through the Praise Pages and back cover, across the back, and up through the second hole. Tie the two ends of the ribbon in a bow at the front of the journal cover. Don't knot the ribbon. You will want to be able to untie the ribbon easily to add new pages. Repeat for the second ribbon and the other two holes.

Use the Praise Journal to log your daily devotional time. Remember, with Jesus as your guide, you'll always be headed in the right direction!

GIFT BOX
PARTY FAVORS

Materials
★ wood (⅛" thick)
★ sandpaper
★ paint and brushes
★ quick-drying craft glue or wood glue
★ gift ribbon, small bows
★ glue
★ scissors
★ paper
★ tissue paper

Make a favor and give it to a friend. Remember Jesus' words: "Freely ye have received, freely give" (Matthew 10:8).

Here's How

1. For each party favor, cut four 2¼" x 2¼" sides and one base (2¼" x 2½") from the wood. Sand all the pieces.

2. Paint the sides of the boxes in gift-wrap designs (See the illustrations below.)

3. When paint is dry, glue the four sides to the base. Butt the sides against each other to fit the base. Glue together along sides.

4. Glue ribbons and bows to each side to resemble a wrapped package.

5. Cut four gift tags from paper, using the pattern provided. Write messages on each tag and glue one on each side of the favor box.

6. Line the box with a square of tissue paper and fill with nuts or candies.

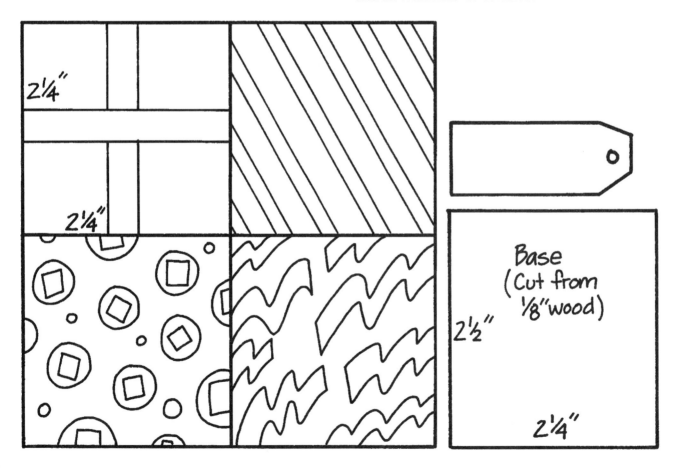

Seashell Party Pals

Materials

★ assortment of seashells (may be purchased at a local craft supply store or pet shop that sells fish supplies)
★ quick-drying craft glue or hot glue gun
★ copies of the party signs (below)
★ movable eyes, small pom-poms, pipe cleaners, etc.
★ toothpicks

Here's How

1. Select seashells which, when glued together, will form a "Party Pal" with a head, feet, ears, etc. Glue the shells together with craft glue or a hot glue gun.

2. Glue on other features using moveable eyes, pom-poms, pipe cleaners, etc.

3. Cut out a party sign and write a praise quotation. Fold the pennant in half and glue it over the end of a toothpick. Create a way for the Party Pal to hold the pennant.

You'll love using your imagination to create these fun knickknacks. The Party Pals can remind you of the times when Jesus walked on the beach, teaching and loving all those who would follow Him.

Materials

★ yarn
★ pencils
★ pipe cleaners
★ scraps of fake fur
★ construction paper
★ copies of add-ons (below)
★ quick-drying craft glue or hot glue gun

Option: add-on items such as miniature sunglasses, guitar, etc., available at local craft or novelty stores

Here's How

1. Choose a small scrap of fake fur. Wrap it around the eraser end of a pencil and glue it in place to form "hair."

2. Wrap a pipe cleaner around the pencil and twist it in the middle. Add a dot of glue to hold in place. Roll the ends to form "hands."

3. Choose and cut out the add-ons, such as glasses and a microphone. Glue these or other decorative features to your pencil.

Hum a tune of praise each time you use your "Singin' His Praise" pencil!

"Rejoice in the Lord always."

"Singin' His Praise"
Pencils

FOLLOW ME PENDANT

Materials

★ wood (⅛" thick)
★ transfer paper
★ medium-line black permanent marking pen and other colored markers or paint and brushes
★ jute rope (two 2' lengths for each pendant)
★ copy of fish pattern
★ sandpaper
★ clear shellac

Here's How

Part A

1. From wood, cut out the pendant using the pattern below. Drill a hole in one end of the pendant. Sand.

2. Use transfer paper to copy the fish pattern onto the wood. Outline the design and letters with the medium-line marking pen. Color or paint the design and background as desired.

3. When dry, use a coat of clear shellac to seal the wood.

Part B

To make the macrame rope for the pendant, follow these directions.

1. Fold the two pieces of 2' jute and put the ends of the jute together. Hold the ends between the thumbs and index finger and while holding the ends, use the other hand to pull gently on the jute to find the center folds of the two pieces of jute.

2. Grasp the center folds and insert, from front to back, through the hole in the wood pendant. This forms a loop. Insert the four ends of the jute through the loop and pull the ends to tighten the knot on the pendant.

3. You are now ready to begin making knots. Follow this procedure:

a. Separate the jute strands and tie an overhand knot in strands 1 and 2 about two inches from where the jute is attached to the pendant. Then tie a knot in strands 3 and 4. (See illustration.)

b. Now tie an overhand knot in strands 2 and 3. (See illustration.)

c. Grasp strands 1 and 2 again and tie six overhand knots, each about one inch apart.

d. Repeat step c with strands 3 and 4.

e. Tie the ends together. Adjust the length of the pendant to the individual. If the rope is too long, cut a little bit off the ends before tying them together.

This pendant will be a reminder and a witness to others that you want to follow Jesus.

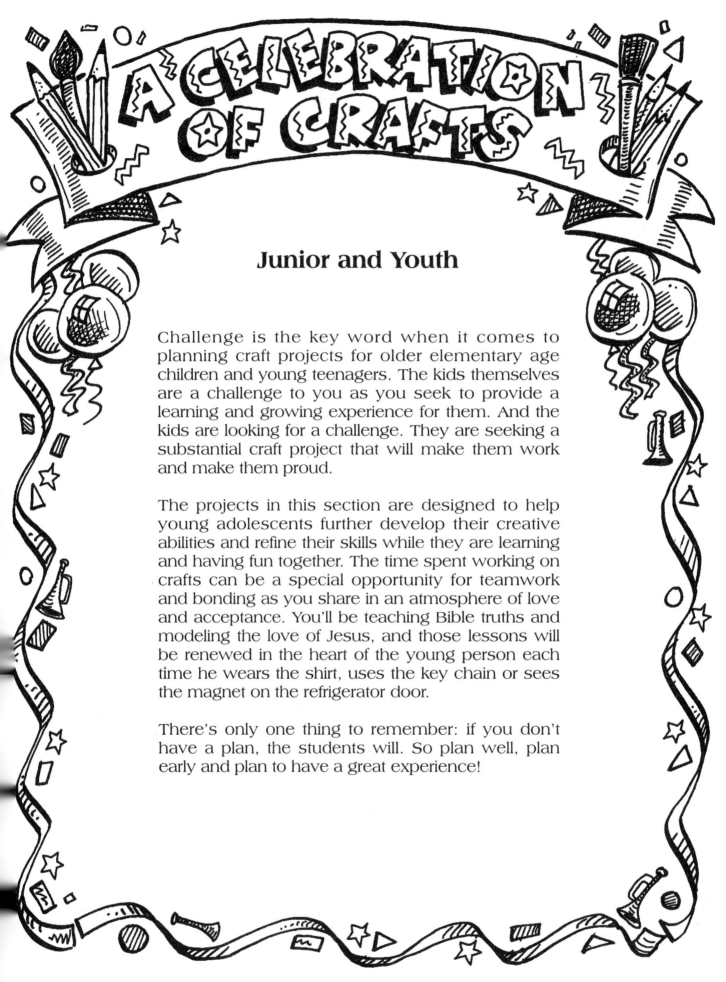

A CELEBRATION OF CRAFTS

Junior and Youth

Challenge is the key word when it comes to planning craft projects for older elementary age children and young teenagers. The kids themselves are a challenge to you as you seek to provide a learning and growing experience for them. And the kids are looking for a challenge. They are seeking a substantial craft project that will make them work and make them proud.

The projects in this section are designed to help young adolescents further develop their creative abilities and refine their skills while they are learning and having fun together. The time spent working on crafts can be a special opportunity for teamwork and bonding as you share in an atmosphere of love and acceptance. You'll be teaching Bible truths and modeling the love of Jesus, and those lessons will be renewed in the heart of the young person each time he wears the shirt, uses the key chain or sees the magnet on the refrigerator door.

There's only one thing to remember: if you don't have a plan, the students will. So plan well, plan early and plan to have a great experience!

WOOD CELEBRATION RACK

Materials:

1 x 6 inch pine board
½ inch diameter wood dowels
Drill with ½ inch bit
Fine-tooth saw
Sandpaper
Hammer
Ruler
Craft knife
Carbon paper

Acrylic paints (bright colors preferred)
Paintbrushes
Newspapers
White glue
Damp paper towels
Clear acrylic spray
Picture hanger with small nail (one for each student)
Pencil (one for each student)
White paper (optional)

Preparing for your students:

Cut one 20" length **pine board** for each student. Cut four 2½" **wood dowels** for each student. On each **pine board**, mark the position for the four peg holes (**See Figure A**). Using a ½" **drill bit**, drill ½" deep peg holes in each board.

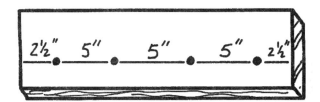

Figure A

Directions:

1. Work in a well-ventilated area.
2. Cover your work surface with **newspaper**.
3. **Sand** the four pegs and the front of the **pine board** until it is smooth.
4. Copy the design provided onto the **rack** with **carbon paper**; or, create your own design on white paper and copy it onto the **pine board** (**See Figure B, page 35**).
5. **Paint** the design.
6. Put several drops of **white glue** into each of the four peg holes. Insert the 2½" **wood dowels** into the holes. Using the **damp paper towel**, wipe off any excess **glue.**
7. Allow the **paint** and **white glue** to dry overnight.
8. **Nail** the **picture hanger** 1" from the top to the center back of the **pine board.**
9. Spray the **Celebration Rack** with **clear acrylic spray**. Allow the **rack** to dry. When it is dry, spray it with a second coat. Your **Celebration Rack** is now complete (**See Figure C**).

Figure C

**Wood
Celebration
Rack
Pattern**

Figure B

PARTY SHIRTS
(TIE-DYED T-SHIRTS)

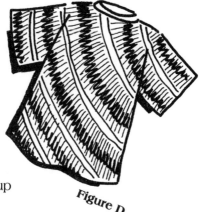

Figure D

Materials:

T-shirt (cotton only)
Empty squeeze bottles (old ketchup, shampoo, conditioner bottles, etc.)
Old dishpan (or something similar in size)
Water

Rubber bands
Dye
Rubber gloves
Glass measuring cup
Iron

Figure A

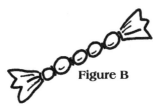

Figure B

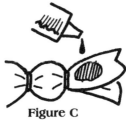

Figure C

Directions:

1. Wash and dry **T-shirt** before tie-dying.

2. Gather the shirt in your hand from the lower edge of the right sleeve to the edge of the neckband (**See Figure A**). Gather tightly with a **rubber band**.

3. Tie the second section like the first, leaving about an inch of shirt between the first **rubber band** and the second. Your shirt should look like **Figure B** when you have finished with the tied sections.

4. For each color of **dye** being used, mix 1 teaspoon of **dye** to 4 teaspoons of **water** in a **glass measuring cup**. Pour each **dye** mixture into your **squeeze bottles**.

5. Begin dyeing the **T-shirt**, working over your **dishpan** at all times. Using the **squeeze bottles**, start squeezing the color you want on the sleeve first. Then move to the next big section of your **T-shirt** with your next bottle of color. Make sure that you do not put **dye** in the rubber banded areas, as they will appear white on your shirt (**See Figure C**).

6. Do not pour too much **dye** onto a section at once, as the **dye** tends to spread quickly and will spread into other sections.

7. In order for **dyes** to remain colorfast, they need to be heat-set. Line dry the **T-shirt** first, then turn it inside out and set the **iron** on cotton setting. Press each dyed area of the **T-shirt** for 20 seconds. Your **T-shirt** is now complete (**See Figure D**).

Celebration Bridge

(A Simple Reminder to Celebrate Jesus!)

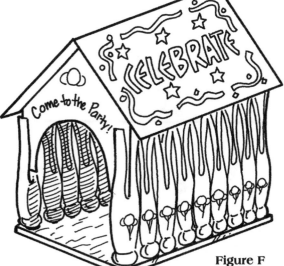

Figure F

Materials:

⅛ inch sheets of wood—you will need 7⅞ inch x 13½ inch piece of wood to cut out 5 pieces (**see Figure A, page 37 for exact sizing**) for each student.
18 flat clothespins for each student
Acrylic paint
Paintbrushes
Water for cleaning paintbrushes
Toothpicks
Clear acrylic spray
Carbon paper
Pencil
Newspaper
White glue
Sandpaper

Preparing for your students:

Cut out the pieces needed for each student from the 7⅞" by 13½" piece of wood: bridge floor (4" x 5"); roof—2 pieces (2¾" x 6"); arches—2 pieces (**See Figure B for exact size and cutting directions**). After cutting the two arches per directions, set aside the half-circles for a keychain and a magnet.

Directions:

1. Sand the **wood** edges smooth with **sandpaper**.

2. Copy the designs provided onto the **wooden pieces** and the **clothespins** with **carbon paper** and **pencil**; or create your own design (**See Figure C, pages 37 & 38**).

3. **Paint** the balloon design (page 38) on the **clothespins**. If the **paintbrushes** are too thick, students may want to paint the designs with **toothpicks** instead. Set the **clothespins** aside to dry.

4. **Glue** the **clothespins** together, two rows of nine **clothespins** each. Set aside to dry (**See Figure D, page 38**). *Note: Whenever gluing is required, pieces may stay in place better if they are held together with tape during the drying process.*

5. **Paint** the designs on the two roof pieces and the two arches with **acrylic paint**. If the students desire, they may paint the bridge floor also. Set the pieces aside to dry.

6. **Glue** the rounded bottoms of the clothespins to the bridge floor (**See Figure E, page 38**). Set aside to dry.

7. Place the arches into the outermost **clothespin** "slots" and **glue** into place (**See Figure E, page 38**). Allow the **glue** to dry.

8. **Glue** the roof pieces to the arches.

9. Your **Celebration Bridge** is now complete. You may want to spray the **bridge** with **clear acrylic spray** (**See Figure F, page 36**).

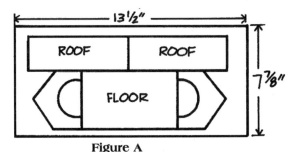

Figure A

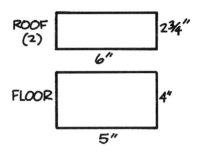

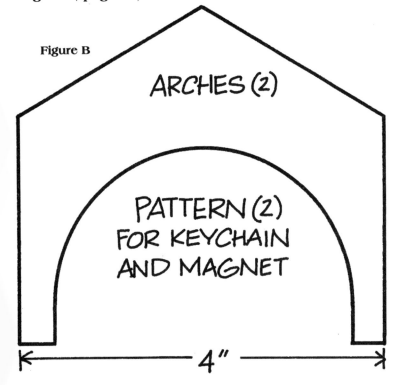

Figure B

ARCHES (2)

PATTERN (2) FOR KEYCHAIN AND MAGNET

◄——— 4" ———►

Figure C

Patterns

Celebration Bridge

Figure E

Figure C

Figure D

Magnet

Keychain

Materials:

1 half-circle from **Celebration Bridge** arch
   (one for each student)
Carbon paper
Pencil
Toothpicks
Clear acrylic spray
Drill

Acrylic paints
Paintbrushes
Newspaper
Water for cleaning paintbrushes
Sandpaper
4 inch bead chain with clasp
   (one for each student)

Preparing for your students:

   Drill a hole in the **half-circle** large enough to thread the **bead chain** through.

Directions:

   1. Sand the **keychain** to smooth the rough edges with **sandpaper**.

   2. Copy the design provided **(See page 38)** onto the **keychain** with **carbon paper** and **pencil**; or, create your own design.

   3. **Paint** the design with **acrylic paints**. If the **paintbrushes** are too thick, students may want to paint the designs with **toothpicks** instead. Allow the paint to dry.

   4. Thread the **4" bead chain** through the hole and close the clasp.

   5. Your **"Rejoicing is the Key!" Keychain** is now complete. You may want to spray the **keychain** with **clear acrylic spray**.

Materials:

1 half circle from **Celebration Bridge** arch (one for each student)
Acrylic paints
Paintbrushes
Newspaper
Sandpaper
Carbon paper

Toothpicks
Magnet strips
Scissors
Water for cleaning paintbrushes
Clear acrylic spray
Pencil

Preparing for your students:

Cut the **magnet strips** into 1" pieces for each student.

Directions:

   1. Sand the **half circle** to smooth the rough edges with **sandpaper**.

   2. Copy the design provided **(See page 38)** onto the **wood half circle** with **carbon paper** and **pencil**; or, create your own design.

   3. **Paint** the design with **acrylic paints**. If the **paintbrushes** are too thick, students may want to paint the designs with **toothpicks** instead. Allow the paint to dry.

   4. Attach the **magnet** to the back of the **half circle**.

   5. Your **"Come to the Party. . .Celebrate Jesus" Magnet** is now complete. You may want to spray the **magnet** with **clear acrylic spray**.

Clothespin Kid

Thanks to Millie Kuhn, Hillsboro, OH for the Clothespin Kid.

Materials:

5 Clothespins for each student
2 small Rubber Bands for each student
Wood bead (outside diameter—1¼" x 1³⁄₁₆";
    inside diameter ¹⁹⁄₃₂" round x ⅜" deep)
Acrylic Paints (white, black, red)
Paintbrushes
Newspapers
Drill
Fine-tooth saw
Colorful Material for shirts and shorts
Yarn (for hair)
Thread
Needles
White glue
#9 or #10 Crochet Hook (an unbent jumbo paper clip
    will work, but not as effectively)

Preparing for your students:

Have a Clothespin Kid with clothes and one without clothes to show your students. You will need to cut the five clothespins with the fine-tooth saw. Follow these directions: (Each clothespin is approximately 3½" long.)

Fig. A: Clothespin Kid

Fig. B: Body (1 clothespin)——Cut off the rounded top of the body clothespin. Cut off ½" from the bottom of the body (both prongs).

Fig. C: Arms (2 clothespins)—Cut off the 1¼" of one prong and 1½" of the other prong.

Fig. D: Legs (2 clothespins)—Cut one prong off 1½". Leave the other prong intact.

Fig. E: Drill holes ¼" from the ends of the longest prongs for the arms and legs. Drill holes ¼" from the top and ¼" from the bottom of the body.

Fig. F

Depending on the time you have allotted for crafts, you may want to glue the 1½" wood bead (head) to the top of the body clothespin. The 1½" hole in the wood bead should fit down over the top of the clothespin. Again, depending on your time, you could paint the arms with white acrylic paint and the legs with black acrylic paint. Using Fig F, make a pattern for the shorts and shirts from newspaper. You may choose to make up the shorts and shirts ahead of time or students may assemble the outfits themselves.

Directions:

1. Glue the 1½" wood bead (head) to the top of the body clothespin. Set aside to dry.

2. Paint the two arm clothespins with white acrylic paint and the two leg clothespins with black acrylic paint. Set aside to dry.

3. Feed the end of one of the small rubber bands through one of the arm holes with the crochet hook. Tie a knot at the end of the rubber band, then push the other end through the top of the body clothespin and the other arm. Tie a knot at that end. (See Fig. A.)

4. Feed the end of the other small rubber band through one of the leg holes with the crochet hook. Tie a knot at the end of the rubber band, then push the other end through the two prongs at the bottom of the body clothespin and the other leg. Tie a knot at that end. (See Fig. A.)

5. Paint a face on the head, add yarn hair or create a hat from material scraps.

6. Cut out the material for shorts and the shirt and sew the Clothespin Kid's wardrobe.

7. Dress the Clothespin Kid (See Fig. F.)

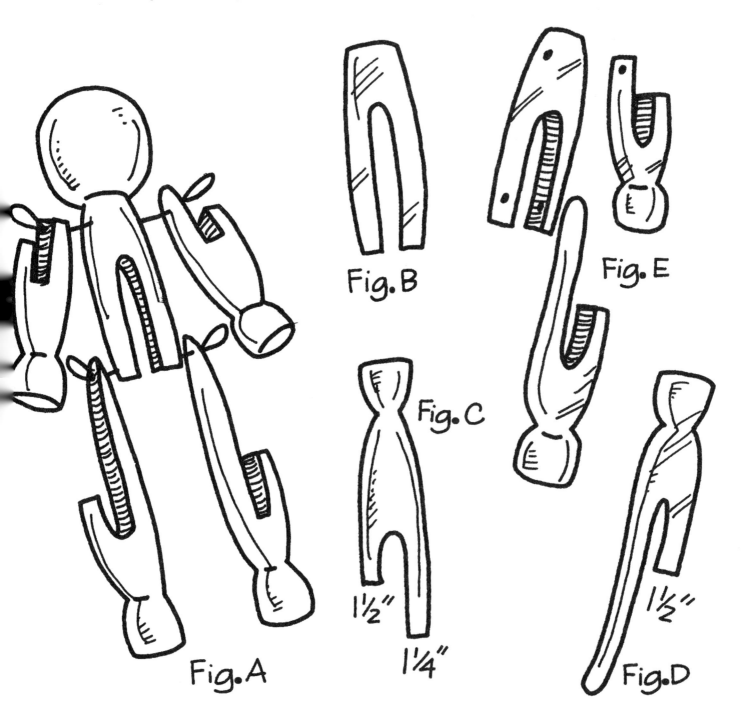

Fig. A

Fig. B

Fig. C

1½"

1¼"

Fig. E

Fig. D

1½"

PARTY FOOD 'N FUN

No party is complete without food and fun!

Choose a recipe or activity and test it out to become familiar with how it works.

Make some great snacks like:
- cheesy popcorn,
- super surprise balls or
- oatmeal cookies.

Try some recipes for classroom fun like:
- homemade paint,
- creative salt art or
- pud. (Pud? What's pud?)

Create a
- balloon person or
- hopping cricket.

Then involve the kids in creating or using these fun-tastic recipes and activities.

Celebrate Jesus!
Share his love!
Share the joy!

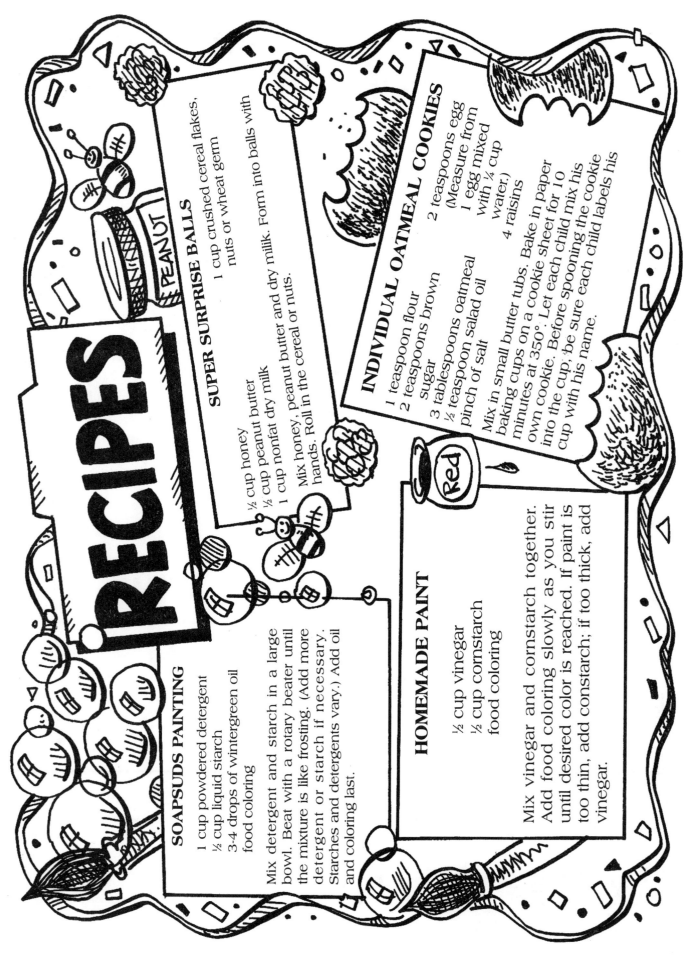

RECIPES

SUPER SURPRISE BALLS

1 cup crushed cereal flakes,
nuts or wheat germ

½ cup honey
½ cup peanut butter
1 cup nonfat dry milk

Mix honey, peanut butter and dry milk. Form into balls with nuts. Roll in the cereal or nuts.

INDIVIDUAL OATMEAL COOKIES

1 teaspoon flour
2 teaspoons brown
  sugar
3 tablespoons oatmeal
½ teaspoon salad oil
  pinch of salt

2 teaspoons egg
  (Measure from
  1 egg mixed
  with ¼ cup
  water.)
4 raisins

Mix in small butter tubs. Bake in paper baking cups on a cookie sheet. Let each child mix his own cookie. Before spooning the cookie into the cup, be sure each child labels his cup with his name. Bake for 10 minutes at 350°.

SOAPSUDS PAINTING

1 cup powdered detergent
½ cup liquid starch
3-4 drops of wintergreen oil
  food coloring

Mix detergent and starch in a large bowl. Beat with a rotary beater until the mixture is like frosting. (Add more detergent or starch if necessary. Starches and detergents vary.) Add oil and coloring last.

HOMEMADE PAINT

½ cup vinegar
½ cup cornstarch
  food coloring

Mix vinegar and cornstarch together. Add food coloring slowly as you stir until desired color is reached. If paint is too thin, add constarch; if too thick, add vinegar.

CHEESY POPCORN

¼ cup cooking oil
⅓ cup popcorn
¼ cup butter or margarine
1 tablespoon cheese
½ cup Parmesan cheese
salt

Pop corn in popper. Melt butter.
Divide popcorn into two or more
paper bags. Let the children use a
teaspoon to sprinkle butter over cheese
popcorn. Then sprinkle with cheese
and salt. Close bag and shake.
Spread on a cookie sheet and place
in the oven for 8-10 minutes.

PUD

½ box cornstarch
water

Pour cornstarch into 13x9-
inch pan. Add water slowly
and stir. Pick it up! Squeeze it!
Watch what happens!

HIPPO FUN

Make blueberry gelatin according to directions.
Pour each serving into a small shallow bowl and
allow to set.

When gelatin is set, arrange pear half on top of each
bowl. Add gumdrop nose and eyes and almond ears.

Then
have
some
hippo
fun!

CREATIVE SALT ART

Add 5-6 drops of food coloring to ½
cup household salt. Shake well. Cook
in microwave oven for 1-2 minutes or
spread on waxed paper and let dry.
Store in an airtight container.

To use colored salt, gather:
• shirt box lids,
• colored salt,
• plastic spoons.
• glue,
• construction paper or pictures and
• plastic tablecloth to cover the floor.

Place picture in shirt box lid in order
to catch any loose salt. Place glue on
area to be covered by salt. Using a
spoonful of salt at a time, sprinkle
salt on the glue. When enough salt is
applied, gently shake box to cover
sand on the glue. Let dry.
glue. Let dry.

NO BAKE
PEANUT BUTTER CANDY

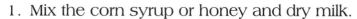

- 2 cups dry milk
- 1 cup corn syrup or honey
- 1 cup peanut butter

1. Mix the corn syrup or honey and dry milk.
2. Let it stand for 20 minutes. (This step is important.)
3. Mix in peanut butter and knead with hands until it is thoroughly mixed and smooth.
4. Roll with hands on wax paper into rope-like lengths.
5. Lengths can vary according to your preference. Wrap ropes in wax paper and chill until firm.

POTATO CANDY

- 1/3 cup mashed potatoes
- peanut butter
- 1 box powdered sugar

Mix powdered sugar with mashed potatoes.

Roll dough out on waxed paper sprinkled with flour.

Spread a layer of peanut butter across mixture.

Roll into log and refrigerate until firm.

Cut in slices and eat!

PARTY CRICKET
'HOP-TO-IT' PAPER PET

1 Begin with a four-inch square of origami paper or strong wrapping paper. Write A B C D in the corners.

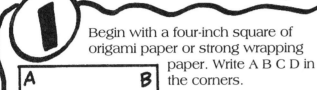

2 Fold the square across the diagonal; color side out. Corner D to corner B. Crease the fold.

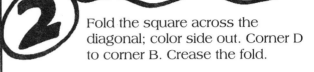

3 Bring corner A up to corner B. Crease the fold. Bring corner C up to corner B. Crease the fold.

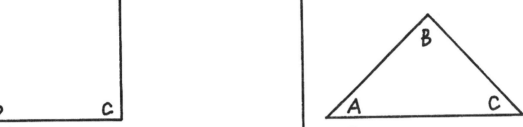

4 Fold corner E to corner F away from you. Crease the fold.

5 Fold corner E to edge BX toward you. Crease the fold. Turn over. Fold corner F to edge BX toward you. Crease the fold.

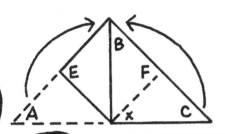
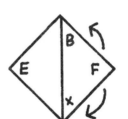

6 Set cricket down on the table with corners E and F flat on the table. Make an eye dot near corner X.

Tap the loose folds (A, B, C). The cricket will do flips!

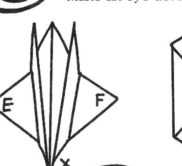

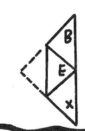

JUMP FOR JOY!

INSTRUCTIONS

1. Blow up a round balloon and tie it.
2. Copy feet on heavy paper or mount feet on cardboard.
3. Cut out feet and cut the two marked lines.
4. Slip balloon knot in to where the two cut lines meet.
5. Decorate the balloon by gluing on cut out eyes, nose, mouth, eyebrows and mustache (optional).
6. Or create your own body parts!

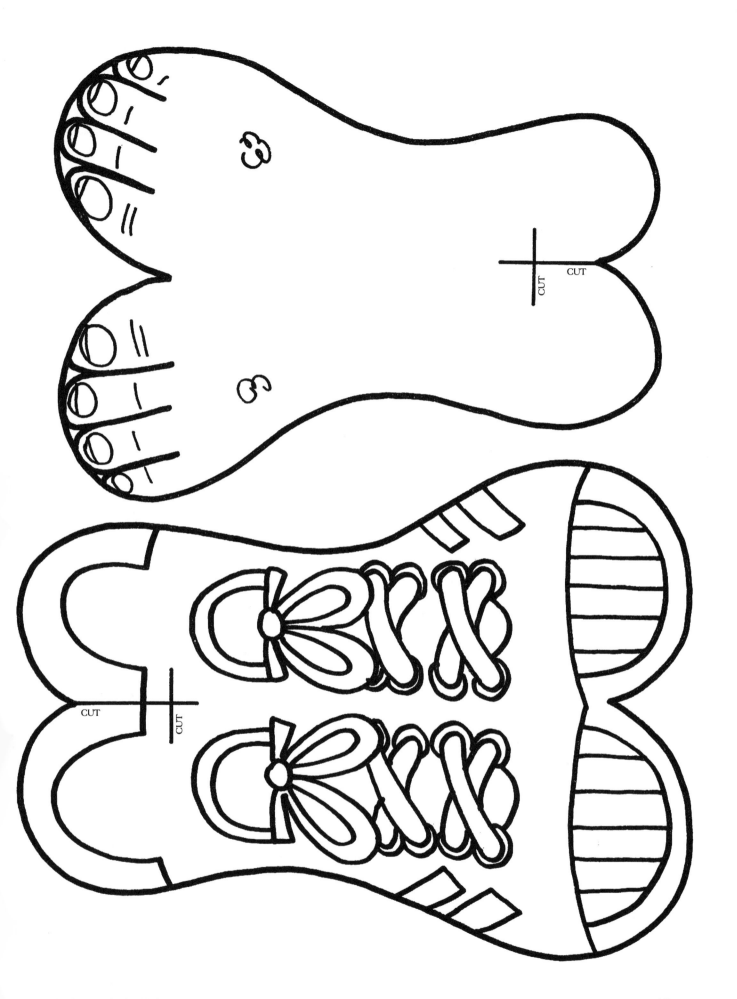

REPRODUCIBLE POSTERS & CERTIFICATES

Here are reproducibles galore to reinforce the joy of walking with Jesus!

You'll find something for all ages—preschool through youth.

- A party alphabet for banners, posters and bulletin boards. Recruit the kids to help color.

- A celebration invitation and hallelujah day note card to send to parents or friends. Invite them to your celebration or write a special message.

- Bookmarks to give as prizes or make for gifts. Laminate them to last a lifetime.

- Posters with Bible truths to color. Frame them to hang.

- Certificates to use as rewards and thank-yous. Personalize them to fit any need.

Hip-hippo-ray! Use these reproducibles lots of ways!

CRAFT PROJECTS

COPIER

INVITATIONS

FUN-TASTIC CRAFTS & FANTASTIC IDEAS

FEATURING:

• FUN CRAFTS

• FANTASTIC REPRODUCIBLES

• FABULOUS FOODS!

YOU'RE GONNA LOVE IT!

STANDARD PUBLISHING
Cincinnati, Ohio